Gaveele

Steve Young

SPORTS REPORTS

Steve Young

Star Quarterback

Ron Knapp

ENSLOW PUBLISHERS, INC.

44 Fadem Road	P.O. Box 38
Box 699	Aldershot
Springfield, N.J. 07081	Hants GU12 6BP
U.S.A.	U.K.

Library of Congress Cataloging-in-Publication Data

Knapp, Ron.
    Steve Young: star quarterback / Ron Knapp.
        p. cm. — (Sports reports)
    Includes bibliographical references and index.
    Summary: Profiles the personal life and football career of the man who
succeeded Joe Montana as quarterback for the San Francisco 49ers.
        ISBN 0-89490-654-2
        1. Young, Steve, 1961– —Juvenile literature. 2. Football players—United
States—Biography—Juvenile literature. 3. San Francisco 49ers (Football
team)—Juvenile literature. [1. Young, Steve, 1961– . 2. Football players.]
    I. Title. II. Series.
GV939.Y69K63 1996
796.332'092—dc20   95-23282
[B]   CIP
                                                                          AC

Printed in the United States of America

10 9 8 7 6 5 4 3 2 1

Photo Credits: AP/Wide World Photos, pp. 25, 33; LDS Archives, p. 13;
© Mitchell Layton, pp. 6, 9, 20, 38, 42, 45, 48, 51, 57, 59, 64, 67, 70, 73, 77, 81,
87, 89, 93, 95.

Cover Illustration: © Mitchell Layton

Contents

For four straight years, superstar quarterback Steve Young was the NFL's top passer.

Chapter 1

The Reward

Steve Young had almost done it all. He was the superstar quarterback of the San Francisco 49ers, one of the best teams in the National Football League. For four straight years he was the NFL's top passer. Twice he had been named the league's most valuable player.

But something important was missing. "Great quarterbacks are judged on how many Super Bowls they've won," said San Diego safety Darren Carrington. "And he hasn't won any."[1]

In the 1995 Super Bowl, Young finally got his chance. He had led the San Francisco 49ers to the big game against the San Diego Chargers. This time his team hadn't folded in the playoff games. This time he was the starting quarterback, not Joe Montana's backup.

Could Steve Young win the Super Bowl? If he didn't, many fans would say he had choked, that he just wasn't as good as Montana. After all, the 49ers had won four Super Bowls with Joe as quarterback. Young could feel the pressure. "We're risking everything," he said. "If we lose? Absolute train wreck."[2] Thousands packed Joe Robbie Stadium in Miami to view the game, and almost a billion more watched on television.

Young was ready for the challenge. On the first play from scrimmage, he hit fullback William Floyd with a 4-yard pass. Then he passed an 11-yarder to wideout John Taylor. On the next play, the other wideout, Jerry Rice, took off across the middle of the San Diego secondary. He turned around to catch a perfect Young pass, then turned on the speed. Nobody touched him! Forty-four yards and a touchdown! With only 1:24 gone, San Francisco led, 7–0. It was the fastest touchdown in Super Bowl history.

The next time the 49ers got the ball, they had a third-down-and-three-yards-to-go situation from their own 28-yard line. Young scrambled for 21 yards and a first down. Then he flung another perfect pass to running back Ricky Watters, who ran over two Chargers on his way to a 51-yard touchdown. "In the first quarter it was like we were a

Young celebrates a TD!

FACT

The Super Bowl has been pro football's championship game since the 1966 season. Originally, it matched the best teams in the National and American Football Leagues. After the two leagues merged into the NFL, the Super Bowl became a contest between the winners of the National Football Conference and the American Football Conferences.

symphony and Steve Young was the conductor," said offensive lineman Jesse Sapolu.[3]

After San Diego scored on a one-yard plunge by Natrone Means, Young marched the 49ers into the end zone again, this time with a 5-yard pass to Floyd.

Before the first half ended, Young connected again with Watters for 8 yards and another touchdown. The 49er lead was 28–7.

By then the fans in Miami and watching on television knew it was all over. The Charger defense would not be able to contain Steve Young and the awesome 49er offense.

In the third quarter, Watters crossed the goal line on a 9-yard run, and Young threw a 15-yard scoring pass to Rice. Just before the superstars left the game for good in the final quarter, Rice caught another TD pass from Young, this one from 7 yards out.

San Francisco buried San Diego, 49–26.

Watters and Rice tied a game record with 3 touchdowns apiece. Rice also set new career marks in touchdowns and reception yardage. Young's 6 Super Bowl touchdown passes were the most ever.

"This one is really special because of Steve Young," Rice said. "Before those final seconds ticked off we just kept hugging each other and I told him, 'Hey, man, I love you. You deserve this. Enjoy it because you will never forget it.'"[4]

Young completed 24 of 36 passes for 325 yards. He also ran for 49 yards. He got every vote for the game's Most Valuable Player. His coach, George Seifert, said he was much more than that. "He's one of the greatest quarterbacks of all time."[5]

In the locker room, Young hugged the championship trophy. "It feels great to win a Super Bowl, throw six touchdowns, and play maybe your best game ever," he said. "It's great to put up the performance we did as a team."[6] He couldn't stop smiling. "I can't describe the feeling. You know, I really wish that anyone who ever played football could feel this."[7]

Chapter 2

Growing Up Mormon

Brigham Young was an early leader of the Mormon Church, a Christian group that began in the 1830s in New England. The Mormons were not popular with their neighbors. They were driven out of several communities, and many of them were killed.

Finally, the Mormons decided to move west, far away from any nonbelievers. In 1847, Young led the first settlers to the Great Salt Lake in what is now Utah. Soon they were joined by many other Mormons. By the time of his death in 1877, Young had brought more than one hundred thousand people to two hundred new settlements around the lake. In 1896, Utah became a state.

Today, Brigham Young University (BYU) in Provo, Utah, honors his memory. The people of the

Brigham Young (1801-1877) led the Mormon settlement of Utah. He had twenty-three wives and forty-seven children. Steve Young is one of his many descendants.

state chose a statue of Young to represent them in the Capitol in Washington, D.C.

There are 7 million Mormons in the world today. Most of them still live in the western United States. Their official name is The Church of Jesus Christ of Latter-Day Saints. Most of them give one tenth of their income to the church. They do not believe in smoking, cursing, or drinking.

LeGrande Young is Brigham Young's great-great-grandson. When he was a star running back at BYU, he was known as "Grit." In 1959, he set the school single-season rushing record.

Jon Steven Young, Grit and Sherry Young's first child, was born on October 11, 1961. Almost right away, the little boy showed that he had inherited his father's love of sports. "One day when I was doing push-ups, Steve, who was only two and a half years old, asked if he could try," said Grit Young. "I said sure, and he got down and did ten of them."[1] When he was three, Steve learned to dribble a basketball. The Youngs moved from Salt Lake City to Greenwich, Connecticut, when Steve was six. Soon he had three brothers and a sister.

By then Grit Young was a corporate lawyer in New York City. He was also a demanding father. "My dad wanted you to do everything perfectly," said Steve, "and he wanted to keep you humble."

FACT

Early Mormons suffered much persecution. Joseph Smith, the church's founder, was murdered by a mob in 1844. The intolerance of the people around them caused the group to keep moving until they reached Utah. One of the main reasons for their unpopularity was their belief in polygamy. Mormons believed that a man should be allowed more than one wife. Brigham Young had twenty-three wives. The church did not outlaw polygamy until 1890, thirteen years after his death.

He expected his children to perform their chores promptly. "He was the kind of guy that when I'd wake up Saturday mornings at, say, nine o'clock and was supposed to mow the lawn, the lawn mower would be going. He would want me to come sprinting out so he could say, 'I can't wait all day.'"[2]

Steve loved his family and liked to stay close to home. "He was one of those kids who could never sleep over at other people's houses because he'd get homesick," said his sister, Melissa. "Steve's friends always came to our house."[3]

As he got older, Steve became an active Boy Scout. "I took part in as many exciting Scout activities as possible," he said. He even began to enjoy campouts away from home. "A highlight was going canoeing in Canada every summer. "I also made Life Scout."[4]

Despite his skill in sports, Steve wasn't always the best athlete in his neighborhood. When he was nine, he played with bigger boys who always picked him last to be on their teams. One of the older kids was a bully who regularly beat him up. Steve didn't hide or run, though. He kept playing, and he got better. His improvement was due in part to the ball camps he attended in the summer. He got lots of practice, and he learned many new skills.

Even as a child Steve hated to lose. Sometimes,

his mother said, he pouted for a whole day after a loss. It was hard for him to accept the fact that losing is a part of sports.[5]

When he was in elementary school, Steve was already dreaming about playing football for Greenwich High School. "My dad always told me not to play football if it wasn't fun," he said. "That's the most important part when you're young."[6]

When he was old enough to play, Steve wasn't an immediate success. "In the tenth grade," he said, "I threw eight interceptions in a junior varsity game. As you can guess, we lost."[7] With practice, Steve improved. "He was a tremendous athlete and he always had a great work ethic, too," said Mike Ornato, his high school coach.[8]

The Greenwich team used a wishbone offense that concentrated on running the ball. Steve couldn't drop back to throw the ball; he had to pass while he was rolling out. That's hard to do, so he usually just kept the ball and ran with it. When he did try to pass, he was usually embarrassed. Even Ornato admitted that his quarterback was a pretty poor passer. In spite of this, Steve was picked as All-County quarterback.

Throwing a football was just about the only athletic skill Steve hadn't picked up by the time he graduated from Greenwich High in 1980. He averaged 20 points a game in basketball. He batted .600 in baseball and was the school's best pitcher. His teammates elected him captain of all three teams.

While becoming a sports star, Steve was also a straight-A student. He had a reputation as a mature, responsible young man. He gave the credit for that to his parents and his religion. Being a Mormon wasn't easy, especially in Connecticut, where very few of his neighbors or friends attended his church. Some of his non-Mormon friends cursed, drank, and smoked. "I had to decide early on what I believed in because I was living something that was hard to live," he said. "Growing up in Connecticut, I used to think there were only four Mormons in the world—my parents, me, and Brigham Young." Steve stuck to his religion. "My friends always respected me, and no human being ever had more fun."[9]

With his fine grades, Steve would have been accepted by almost any college in the country. He didn't need an athletic scholarship, but he had begun to think about a college football career. Despite his athletic success in high school, he was recruited only by the University of North Carolina. They were thinking of moving him from quarterback to running back.

Steve talked LaVell Edwards, the BYU coach, into giving him a chance to play at his father's old school. The Cougars were known for their strong passing attack, and Edwards didn't think Steve could throw. An assistant coach told him that if he made the team, he would probably have to play in the defensive backfield.

Steve decided to attend the school named after his great-great-great-grandfather, and he convinced the coaching staff to give him a chance at being a quarterback. In the fall of 1980, when he arrived in Provo, he was listed as BYU's eighth-string quarterback. The first time he touched the ball at practice, he dropped back, tripped over his feet, and fell down. His teammates were not impressed. Most of them were laughing.[10]

Steve got up and tried again. He knew he had a long way to go.

Chapter 3

All-American Cougar

Steve Young practiced hard during his freshman year at Brigham Young University, but nobody seemed to notice. The coaches were much more interested in the team's other quarterbacks. They didn't even bother giving him much advice. What he learned he picked up from watching Jim McMahon, the Cougars' star quarterback. "I learned to throw at Brigham Young, mostly from Jim McMahon," he said. "It was really good for me."[1]

During the first season, Young never touched the game ball. When it was over, the coaches told him he just wasn't good enough to play quarterback for a major college like BYU. Sure, he was a great athlete, but unless he switched positions, he wasn't going to get much game time. They suggested he become a defensive back. Instead of throwing his

Steve, as a 49er, demonstrates his throwing style.

own passes, he would be trying to intercept passes thrown by the other team's quarterbacks.

That wasn't what Young had in mind when he left Connecticut for Provo. He wanted to be the starting quarterback at a big-time school, the same one his dad had played for in the 1950s. If he couldn't play quarterback, he decided, he was going to quit football. His father thought that was a terrible idea. "You can quit," he told his son, "but you can't live here."[2]

Grit Young wanted his son to stick it out and stay with the team. The first year at college is tough for almost everybody. In class, freshmen who got great grades in high school are surprised to be surrounded by other hardworking, intelligent students. They're not always the smartest people anymore. It's the same thing on the football field. Athletes who were superstars in high school discover that their college teammates are excellent players, too.

Young's father wanted him to move to the defensive backfield as his coaches suggested. Maybe by the time he was a senior, he would be a starter, or at least he might get some playing time. Then he would leave football behind, graduate, and get a good job. Young finally agreed to return to Provo.

In the summer of 1981, Steve Young went back

FACT

More than twenty-five thousand students attend Brigham Young University in Provo, Utah. Almost all of them are Mormon. The campus sits in front of the snowcapped Uinta Range of the Rocky Mountains in central Utah, about forty miles south of Salt Lake City. It's traditional for seniors to pose for a graduation photograph sitting on the statue of a cougar that is outside the football stadium.

to BYU. Ted Tollner, the team's quarterback coach, told Young he "could switch to the secondary and play or stay at quarterback and be on the bench behind Jim McMahon." Young's answer was the same: "I want to be a quarterback."[3]

Then, at an early practice, one of his coaches was finally impressed by the way he was throwing the ball. He asked Head Coach LaVell Edwards to watch. It didn't take them long to decide that Young deserved another chance at being a quarterback. "All I wanted was a shot," he said. "I thought I could throw. I just wanted a chance to do it. If I didn't make it after that, I would have played defensive back, receiver, running back, wherever they needed me."[4]

Once he got his shot, Young proved he could do the job. By the time the season opened, he was the number two quarterback behind McMahon. He even got on the field for 11 plays against California-Long Beach. He passed 8 times, completing 5 for 47 yards. He also got a chance to show that he could run with the ball. In three carries, he picked up 15 yards. As soon as he stepped on the field he made Cougar history, just as his father had done twenty-two years before. Steve was the school's first left-handed quarterback.

Young had a few plays in each of BYU's next

three victories, but McMahon was still the star. Young didn't figure he'd see a lot of action until the star graduated; but then a knee injury put McMahon on the bench, and Young took over. The team's sixteen-game winning streak was on the line against Utah State. He connected with his receivers 21 times for 307 yards as he led the Cougars to a 32–26 win.

McMahon was still out of action the following week, so Young started against Nevada-Las Vegas. Again he completed 21 passes, this time for 269 yards, but UNLV broke the BYU winning streak with a 45–41 victory.

Young was back on the bench as soon as McMahon's knee healed. In the last six games, he was only on the field for thirteen plays, but he had shown what he could do. McMahon's last year at BYU was 1981. After that, the quarterback's job belonged to Steve Young.

In the first game of his junior season, Young completed 19 of 26 passes for 271 yards against UNLV. But the next week, the Georgia secondary intercepted six of his passes and BYU fell, 17–14. Then came the first game in the Cougars' newly expanded stadium. More than sixty thousand fans saw his team lose to Air Force, 39–38. The fans began to wonder: Was Young really good enough to be leading BYU? "There were times that I questioned myself in those early days," he said. "But I convinced myself that a throwing football team will make mistakes, and that I had to keep plugging away."[5]

His 399 passing yards helped the Cougars beat Texas-El Paso, 51–3. That was the first of seven straight Western Athletic Conference victories in which he threw for more than 200 yards. The Cougars won the WAC title and earned a spot in the Holiday Bowl against Ohio State. Unfortunately, the season ended disastrously, as BYU lost, 47–17.

Young's great season won him honors as the WAC Offensive Player of the Year. He finished with 3,100 passing yards good for 18 touchdowns. He completed 230 of 367 passes. He also got plenty of chances to run, compiling 407 yards and 10 touchdowns in 114 carries.

Young had one more season, and he wanted to make the most of it. "I love practice," he said. "I can't wait to go back out each day. It never gets monotonous. It's a constant challenge. . . . And as long as I work hard, I think my play will continue to improve."[6]

In the first game of the 1983 season, Young rushed for 113 yards and passed for 351, but BYU lost to Baylor, 40–36. After that, he led the Cougars to eleven straight wins. Against Air Force, he

FACT

During his three years of playing quarterback for BYU, Steve Young completed 65.2 percent of his passes, still a major college record. Another BYU star, Ty Detmer, now has the career records for completed passes (958) and yards (15,031). Detmer played for the Cougars from 1988 to 1991.

In 1983 Young set an NCAA record in this game against the U.S. Air Force Academy. He passed for 18 consecutive completions in the game.

completed 18 straight passes, setting an NCAA record, finishing with 486 yards and 3 touchdowns.

The University of California at Los Angeles (UCLA) was so worried about Young's passing that they only had four men on the line of scrimmage. They used most of their defense to cover the Cougars' receivers. This opened the way for the Cougar backs to run for 265 yards. Despite the seven Bruins playing back, Young still passed for 270 yards. He totaled 446 yards and 5 scores (3 passing, 2 running) against San Diego State. Then he destroyed Utah with 6 touchdown passes.

When the season was over, Young was named to almost every All-America team. In the Heisman Trophy balloting, he finished second, after Nebraska's Mike Rozier.

By then he had made it into the record books in many categories besides those for left-handed passing. His season total of 4,346 offensive yards was 1,303 better than anybody else in Division 1-A. BYU had averaged 395.1 rushing and passing yards per game, an National Collegiate Athletic Association record. "Young did it because he can run like a halfback," said Jim Van Valkenburg, the NCAA director of statistics. "He gained 623 running and scrambling, lost 179 on sacks for a net of 444 rushing."[7] Those 444 rushing yards were eleven better

FACT

The Heisman Trophy is awarded each season to the nation's best college football player. After the 1983 season, Steve Young finished second in the balloting to Nebraska's Mike Rozier. Other winners have included Doug Flutie, Bo Jackson, Barry Sanders, and Desmond Howard.

than his dad's 1959 record-setting total as a running back.

Young had proved that he was an extremely accurate passer. His receivers caught 306 of the 429 passes he threw, for a completion rate of 71.3 percent.

During his years at BYU, he also kept up on his studies, earning a B average while majoring in accounting and international relations. That earned him honors as an Academic All-American and as a National Football Hall of Fame Scholar Athlete. He had hoped to find a good job after graduating; maybe he could even go on to law school and become an attorney like his father.

After his terrific college football career, though, Young knew he wouldn't soon be looking for a regular job or thinking about law school. For a few years, at least, he wanted to earn big money as a professional quarterback. In the winter of 1984, he waited to see which teams wanted him.

Chapter 4

A Chance with the USFL

Ever since Steve Young was a kid, he had dreamed of playing in the National Football League. His favorite player was Roger Staubach, the great Dallas Cowboys quarterback.

In the 1984 draft, he was taken by the Cincinnati Bengals, which meant that they were the only NFL team that could offer him a contract. There was a team in another league that wanted him, too—the Los Angeles Express of the United States Football League. Young was lucky. The USFL was trying to sign all the stars that the NFL wanted. They were in a bidding war. Young and his agent, Leigh Steinberg, waited to see which team would offer him the most money.

The Cincinnati Bengals came up with an incredible offer—$4 million for four years. Not bad for a twenty-two-year-old who had never held a regular full-time job! Young probably wouldn't get a chance to play much in his first couple of seasons, but the Bengals assured him after that he could earn a starting job. His dreams seemed to be coming true. Soon he would be a millionaire star quarterback in the NFL.

The USFL and the Express wanted Young, too. They figured that if they could sign enough top players, their league would soon become as popular as the NFL. William Oldenburg, the owner of the Express, was willing to spend big money to get Steve Young.

For several days, Steinberg and Grit Young negotiated with the Los Angeles team. When it seemed that they were close to an agreement, Steve Young and Steinberg flew to Oldenburg's office in San Francisco. They were greeted by an electric sign that said "WELCOME, STEVE YOUNG, QUARTER-BACK EXTRAORDINAIRE!"

Then the negotiations ran into a snag. Oldenburg was willing to give Young plenty of money, but he wanted to spread out payments over many years. Steinberg said that his client was willing to wait for some of his money, but he demanded a big lump sum as soon as the contract was signed.

Wasn't it enough, the owner asked in frustration,

FACT

Each spring, the NFL teams have a meeting to choose, or draft, college players. The teams with the worst records get to pick before the better teams. The best players, of course, are taken first. Recent number one draft choices have included John Elway, Bruce Smith, Bo Jackson, and Troy Aikman.

that he was willing to pay him much more money than the Bengals would? No, the agent answered. He wanted to be sure that Young got a lot of money right away. Finally, Oldenburg got mad. "You want guarantees?" he yelled as he wadded up a pile of large bills and threw them at Young and Steinberg. "Here's all the guarantees you'll need."[1]

Young didn't like Oldenburg's attitude. What was wrong with wanting to be paid right away? When Young wouldn't give in, the owner jabbed a finger into his chest and yelled again. By then, the young quarterback had had enough. "If you touch me one more time," he said, "I'll deck you."[2]

Soon the negotiations were over. Oldenburg had his security guards throw Steve Young and his agent out of the building. Young wondered if maybe he would be playing in the NFL after all. Soon Oldenburg calmed down, and finally he agreed on a contract with Steinberg. As soon as the papers were signed, Young was given a $2.5-million check by his new boss. By then, he was sick of the money and the negotiations. He handed the check to his agent and said, "You take it. I don't want it."[3]

There was a lot more to the contract than just one check. Young's yearly salary would range from $300,000 to $600,000 over the next four years. Then, in the thirty years after 1997, Oldenburg would pay him an additional $37.2 million. Young didn't forget his college; the agreement gave Brigham Young University $183,000 to set up a scholarship fund.

The contract was big news across the country. Suddenly a college kid from Connecticut was the highest-paid athlete in the history of team sports. Hardly anybody wanted to talk about Young's accomplishments at BYU or about what he hoped to do for the Express. People wondered if hiring him had been a smart move for the USFL. How could one man be worth all that money?

Young tried to ignore the controversy. Even though he was now a millionaire, he headed back to Provo to finish his spring classes. He still wanted to graduate with the rest of his class.

While he was at BYU, the USFL began playing its spring schedule. By the time his classes were done, the Express had already played six games. Young wasn't even sure he wanted to report to the team. He didn't like dealing with Oldenburg, and he was tired of all the talk about his big money deal. For a while, he even thought about calling it off and refusing to play in the USFL.[4] His father reminded him that he had made a deal and that he had to live up to it. As an attorney, Grit knew that his son was legally obligated to report to Los Angeles.

So Steve became a part of the Express. In two

years with the USFL, he completed 316 of 560 passes for 4,102 yards and 16 touchdowns. His best day came on April 20, 1985, when he became the first pro player to rush for 100 yards and pass for another 300 in the same game.

Even as he played, the Express and the USFL were unraveling because they were running out of money. When players were injured, the teams didn't have the cash to hire replacements. In one game, Los Angeles ran out of running backs, and Young had to move to tailback.

When the Express didn't pay its hotel bill, the players were kicked out and had to find places to stay on their own. Once, their bus driver pulled over to the side of the road on the way to a game and refused to go on unless he was paid. The players had to take up a collection.

After a while, it was hard to take the USFL seriously. Sometimes, Young just wanted to have some fun. Once on the way out of the huddle, he told his center, "Hey, snap it over my head. Let's make something happen."[5]

Young decided that two years in the USFL were enough. He wanted to play in a real league, but first he had to get out of his contract with the Express. He paid the team $1.2 million so that he could leave. Then he turned to the NFL.

FACT

The National Football League wasn't always the only professional football league. From 1960 until 1969, there was the American Football League (AFL), which eventually merged with the NFL. The World Football League only lasted a season and a half (1974–75), while the United States Football League had games from 1983 until 1985. Both the WFL and USFL ran out of money and collapsed. Steve Young was one of many players who switched leagues.

Steve Young scrambles for first down in a game against the Houston Gamblers.

The Bengals no longer had rights to Young. He had been drafted again in 1984 by the Tampa Bay Buccaneers, so he and his agent began negotiating with them. It didn't take long to settle on a six-year deal for $5.4 million.

At last Young would be a quarterback in the NFL. He had left the USFL just in time; soon after he signed with the Buccaneers, the league folded. The Express was finished, and Steve Young was on his way to being a star with a new team.

Chapter 5

Struggling in the NFL

The Tampa Bay Buccaneers were at the bottom of their division when Steve Young joined them, and they didn't get any better during his two seasons with them.

Coach Leeman Bennett wanted his quarterback to drop back after the snap and throw from the pocket, but that wasn't Young's style. He liked to throw while he was running or take off and run the ball himself. Bennett wouldn't let him.

Instead, Young had to back up and look for receivers. He had to look fast because his line couldn't hold off the defense. Almost as soon as he planted his feet and started gazing downfield, he was surrounded by the opposition. With no time to throw, Young gave up 8 interceptions in the five games he played in 1985. He was only able to complete 52.2 percent of his passes.

The next season wasn't much better. His completion rate was 53.7 percent, and he was intercepted 13 times. In fourteen games, he only threw for 8 touchdowns. Young hated playing for a losing team. "I saw what it's like for your season to be over at Halloween," he said. "You know it's not going to get any better."[1]

Despite Bennett's strategy and all the losses, Young kept trying, but many of his teammates got discouraged and gave up. "One time we were playing the Bears," he said, "and one of our coaches looked me right in the eye and said, 'Look, Steve, I know everybody's kind of quit on you here. This is the kind of game where you could really get hurt. Be careful out there.' I couldn't believe it. How can you enter a game thinking like that?"[2]

Young was miserable. Sure, he was making big money, but he wasn't able to show what he could do on the football field. His coach wouldn't let him run, his line couldn't hold off the defense, and many of the other Buccaneers had given up. This was hardly what he had in mind when he had dreamed of being a quarterback in the NFL. "I played in Tampa Bay," he remembered years later. "I played on a team where you have nowhere to go."[3]

Young knew he had to get away from the Buccaneers. "What Steve needed for his career to go to the next level was to be exposed to some top NFL coaching," said Steve DeBerg, his teammate at Tampa Bay. "I told him the perfect place for him was San Francisco with Bill Walsh."[4]

The 49ers were one of the most succcessful teams in the league. While the Buccaneers were 4–28 during Young's two seasons with them, San Francisco had fought its way into the playoffs with a combined record of 20–13–1. With Walsh coaching, they had won Super Bowls in 1981 and 1984.

Steve Young would have loved to play for another team, especially one as good as San Francisco, but he had a long-term contract with Tampa Bay. The team had no intention of letting him buy himself out, so he was stuck.

While he was with the Bucs, Young had other things on his mind besides football. He began to think about his future. Even though he was rich enough never to have to work after his athletic career was over, he knew he wanted to be busy with a new, interesting job. He decided to follow his father and become an attorney. Steve's undergraduate grades were good enough to get him into Brigham Young University's law school. During the off-season he took classes in Provo.

Joe Montana is thought by many sports fans to be the greatest quarterback in the history of the NFL. When Steve joined the 49ers in 1987, Montana had already led the team to two Super Bowl victories.

When he was on campus, he often took part in spring practice with the Cougar team. Bill Walsh was there to watch in 1987. For years, the 49er coach had followed Young's career with BYU, the Express, and Tampa Bay. He knew why Young was doing so poorly with the Bucs. "Tampa couldn't protect the passer," he said, "plus they were running a dated offense."[5]

Walsh liked Young well enough to want him for the 49ers. The team began talking with the Buccaneers about a trade. San Francisco had to give Tampa Bay $1 million and two top draft picks. On April 24, 1987, Young became a San Francisco 49er.

His new job was hardly perfect. The 49ers didn't need a starting quarterback; all they wanted was a backup. They already had Joe Montana, the man many experts thought was the finest quarterback in the league. Montana had led the team to a pair of Super Bowl victories; he was the man the fans filled Candlestick Park to see.

Young knew he'd have to earn any playing time he got. "I guess I looked at it like, if I was going to see how good I was, I was going to see it here," he said. "I mean, the cold, hard truth was going to be known by playing in San Francisco. And I guess I was drawn to it in a weird way."[6] He looked forward to the challenge, and he figured that anything was better than another losing season in Tampa Bay.

FACT

Joe Montana played in four Super Bowls, and the San Francisco 49ers won them all. Montana has the Super Bowl career records for most completed passes (83), touchdown passes (11), and passing yards (1,142). He also has the single-game marks for yards (357) and TD passes (5).

Chapter 6

On the Sidelines

Steve Young spent almost all of his first season in San Francisco watching the great Joe Montana direct the 49er offense. That wasn't much fun. Sometimes he wondered if he was good enough to lead the team himself. Coach Bill Walsh said, "Steve was pretty shaken up related to his self-confidence and shaken up as to what he might be able to accomplish on a football field."[1]

Montana took the team to seven wins in their first eight games. Then he injured his throwing hand, and Young got to start against the New Orleans Saints. It felt great to be back on the field, and at first everything went well. Young completed 5 of 6 passes. One of them was a 46-yard TD toss to Jerry Rice. Four times he took the ball himself, running for a total of 24 yards. Before the first quarter had ended, Young had been knocked flat by a tackler. He had to be helped off the field, and the doctors later told him he had suffered a concussion. Steve Bono, the number three quarterback, had to take over. San Francisco lost, 26–24.

A month later, when Montana pulled a hamstring muscle, Young was back on the field again. This time he didn't get hurt, and he threw 4 touchdown passes as the 49ers crushed the Chicago Bears, 41–0. That was his first big game for San Francisco. After Montana's hamstring healed, Young had no idea when he would play again.

Then, in the National Football Conference Divisional Playoff Game on January 9, 1988, the 49ers were in trouble. The Minnesota Vikings had taken the lead, and Montana was having trouble moving the team. Walsh decided to give Young a try in the third quarter. When Young had trouble spotting receivers, he relied on his running. He got 72 yards and scored on a 5-yard run, but that wasn't enough. Minnesota won, 36–24.

In his first year with the 49ers, Young had completed 37 of 69 passes for 935 yards and 10 touchdowns. He also gained 190 yards in 26 rushing tries. "Steve Young had shown that he had the ability to be the 49er quarterback," Walsh said.

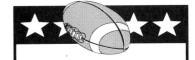

FACT

The San Francisco 49ers have been one of the most successful teams in the NFL. Since 1981, San Francisco has appeared in eight NFC Championship Games and has won five Super Bowls. Only the Dallas Cowboys and the Pittsburgh Steelers have that many Super Bowl victories.

Coach Bill Walsh believed in Steve Young and helped him become a better quarterback.

"Whenever he'd played as a 49er, he'd been not only productive but exciting."[2]

Sitting on the bench wasn't Young's idea of an NFL career. During the season he rented a room from 49er tackle Harris Barton, who was surprised when he borrowed a pair of socks. "I went into his room . . . looked in the drawer and found thirteen uncashed paychecks."

Young said, "I haven't done anything to earn those checks, so I'm not going to cash them until I do."[3]

Coach Walsh didn't care about the checks, but he wanted Young to become a better quarterback—just in case he made it into the games. Walsh wasn't always pleased to see his backup quarterback take the ball. Sometimes Young didn't try hard enough to find a receiver. Instead of taking a few extra seconds to look, he liked to run the ball himself.

On October 30, 1988, Montana had back spasms and was unable to play. Young would start at quarterback against the Minnesota Vikings. Many of the 49er fans were afraid their team was in trouble. The Vikings would be tough; they had knocked the 49ers out of the playoffs in 1987. San Francisco's record in 1988 was now 5–3. If they were going to make it back to the playoffs, they couldn't afford another loss, but did they really have a chance without Montana?

The first half didn't go well for the 49ers. Young was paying so much attention to linebacker Chris Doleman and the rest of the Vikings' pass rush that he wasn't watching his own receivers. It seemed to Young that Doleman was in his face every time he tried to pass the ball.

"But in the second half," Walsh said, "Steve settled down and played well."[4] He engineered a 97-yard drive that gave San Francisco the first touchdown of the third quarter. Then he hit wide receiver John Taylor with a pass that was good for 73 yards and another touchdown.

Late in the fourth quarter, Minnesota led 21–17. The 49ers had the ball at the Viking 49-yard line. It was third down and two yards to go. Walsh told Young to throw a short pass, but when he faded back, all he could see was the Minnesota pass rush closing in on him.

"I moved left to see if a receiver was open," Young said. "But everyone was covered. So I decided to run for the first down."[5] He went up the middle as a pair of Vikings closed in on him.

Tom Rathman, San Francisco's fullback, saved the play by blocking both Minnesota players out of the way. Young had the first down—and he was still running!

He picked up speed and ran past two more

With no receiver in sight, Young runs with the ball.

Vikings, then he headed for the sidelines. "I was going to run out of bounds," he said. That would stop the clock and give the 49ers plenty of time to score on another play. "But someone made another block so I cut to the middle of the field at the thirty."[6]

Young's teammates had raced downfield with him, and they kept blocking Vikings out of the way. Seven Minnesota players had a shot at tackling him, but none of them could. Finally, after dashing back and forth down the field, Young ran out of steam around the 5-yard line and began to stagger. Then, just before going down, he dove over the goal line for the touchdown! The crowd in Candlestick Park screamed their approval as Young's teammates mobbed him in the end zone. When Minnesota couldn't score, and time ran out, the 49ers won, 24–21. His incredible run had won the game.

The president of NFL Films, Steve Sabol, said, "We called that run the best in football over the last twenty-five years."[7] For the first time, Young was named National Football Conference offensive player of the week.

Young was still just a second-string player. After the Minnesota game, not much more was heard about him that season. Montana's back healed, and he was at the peak of his form. The 49ers went into the playoffs with a 10–6 record. They eliminated the

Vikings, 34–9, and dropped the Bears, 28–3. Then Montana earned his third Super Bowl ring by taking San Francisco to a 20–16 win over the Cincinnati Bengals.

George Seifert took over as the 49er coach at the beginning of the 1989 season, but the spotlight, of course, remained on Montana. Young played in just ten games, usually when the outcome had already been decided and Seifert wanted to rest Montana. He started against the Dallas Cowboys and rushed for 79 yards, more than any of the 49er backs, as San Francisco won, 31–14.

When Montana hurt his ribs at Atlanta, Young came off the bench and completed his first 10 passes. He scored on a one-yard touchdown plunge and got another on a 38-yard pass to Taylor. The 49ers won, 23–10. Two weeks later, they beat the Buffalo Bills, 21–10, with Young as the starting quarterback. He put two scores on the board, one with a pass, the other with a short run.

Then Montana took over again, and he was brilliant. At the end of the regular season, San Francisco was 14–2. They overpowered Minnesota, 41–13, and whipped the Los Angeles Rams, 30–3. The Super Bowl was no contest, as they beat the Denver Broncos, 55–10. That game was so far out of reach that Montana rested, and Young got to play

In 1989, George Seifert took over as coach of the 49ers.

in the closing minutes. He got an 11-yard run and completed 2 of 3 passes.

In 1990, the 49ers were aiming for their third straight championship. Young didn't get a start until the season was almost over. On December 23, with his team's playoff spot already secure, Montana stayed on the sidelines. That day Young got 102 yards rushing, but San Francisco was beaten by the Saints, 13–10.

He did much better in the next game against the Vikings. After taking over for Montana in the second half, he drove the 49ers to a come-from-behind touchdown in the final quarter. During that final drive, he completed 6 of 7 passes for 88 yards. The last one was good for 34 yards and the winning touchdown to Taylor. San Francisco had a 20–17 triumph.

With Montana calling the signals, the team beat the Washington Redskins, 28–10, in the first round of the playoffs. Then the 49ers' dreams of three Super Bowl wins in a row melted away when they ran into the New York Giants. Even Montana couldn't move the ball. Young came in briefly near the end of the game, and he couldn't do much, either. The Giants prevailed, 15–13, and the 49ers were eliminated from postseason play.

By the end of the 1990 season, Young had been

in San Francisco for four years. He had spent most of his time standing on the sidelines, waiting for a chance to play, a chance that rarely came. He had started just ten games and had thrown for only 23 touchdowns.

The 49er coaching staff kept insisting that Steve was one of the top quarterbacks in the league. Besides being a great passer, he was also an excellent runner. He would be a starter on almost any NFL team.

Young was afraid that his talent might never win him a starting spot with San Francisco. Montana was a legend who had won the Super Bowl four times. He had earned the right to be the 49ers' starting quarterback. As long as he stayed healthy, he would be the man calling the signals.

Young was getting restless. He kept working hard in practice, hoping that someday he would get a real chance to earn a spot in the starting lineup. Montana didn't like the idea that Young wanted some playing time. He didn't want to share the spotlight. "Steve is on a big push for himself," he said. "And anytime you have a competition, there is always that certain amount of animosity toward each other. I can say we have only a working relationship. That's all it is. After that, he's on my team, but as far as I'm concerned, he's part of the opposition. He wants what I have."[8]

Young tried to keep his good humor during the many months of waiting to get his chance.

Reporters tried to get Young to respond, to say something bad about Montana, but he always refused. "He's been as successful as anyone that's ever played the game," he said. "Under tremendous pressure, he was always level-headed about everything. I admired him for that."[9]

Just because he didn't bad-mouth the man who played ahead of him, this didn't mean that Young was happy with the situation in San Francisco. "My mission ever since I got here was to be ready to play spectacular football, not just substitute football," he said.[10] He was twenty-nine years old, and he knew he didn't have much time left to prove himself. Did he really want to spend the rest of his career on the bench? "I just wanted to get on the field," he said. "I just couldn't take it anymore."[11]

His agent, Leigh Steinberg, suggested that he ask to be traded. He could be a first-string quarterback on almost every other team in the NFL. During the off-season, while he continued to attend classes at the Brigham Young University law school, he wondered if he should try to leave the 49ers.

It wasn't an easy decision, but Young finally figured out that he was better off in San Francisco. He liked the town, and he liked the way the team was run. If he got a chance to play regularly, he was sure that he could be a star. The only thing he didn't like about the 49ers was that he wasn't playing enough, but he had already invested four years of his career with the team. Did he really want to start all over with another team? No; he wanted to be part of the 49ers.[12]

Young would stay with the team. Someday, somehow, he hoped that he would leave the sidelines for good. As the 1991 season approached, he didn't realize it, but his big chance was coming.

Chapter 7

A Chance at Last

For the San Francisco 49ers, the 1990 season had been a disappointment. After two straight Super Bowl victories, their fans had begun to expect nothing but championships. In 1990, the 49ers had won 15 games, but that wasn't good enough to get them to the Super Bowl.

The 1991 season was supposed to be a different story. Montana and the rest of the team were eager to earn another championship ring, but then the veteran quarterback asked the team doctors to take a look at the sore elbow of his throwing arm. It didn't seem like a big deal; Montana expected it to be nothing worse than a sprain.

The 49ers were stunned when the doctors diagnosed a torn tendon in the elbow. Montana had to give it time to heal; the worst thing he could do would be to throw a football. San Francisco's star would be out of action for several weeks, maybe the entire season.

Finally, the spotlight would be on Steve Young. His years of waiting were about to pay off. "Part of the crazy drive about being here and not wanting to go elsewhere, even as Joe kept going and going, was that there is a benchmark of championships here that there is nowhere else," he said later. "I just want to keep that tradition going. That's the real test for me."[1]

In the first game, Young and the 49ers faced the New York Giants, the team that had knocked them out of the 1990 playoffs. Young tried not to run much. Instead, he stayed in the pocket and threw, just the way Montana would have done. He tossed a 73-yard touchdown pass and scored himself on a 5-yard run, but it wasn't enough. New York won, 16–14.

In the next week, Young was the star, completing 26 of 38 passes for 348 yards, as San Francisco dropped San Diego, 34–14. Then he ran into the Minnesota Vikings, and his team was stopped three times inside the 20-yard line. He passed for 2 touchdowns, but the Vikings triumphed, 17–14.

By then, many of the San Francisco fans were complaining about Young's performance. Jerry

FACT

Jerry Rice is the greatest receiver in San Francisco 49er history. He holds nineteen team records for scoring and receiving. He has more than 124 touchdowns, more than twice as many as any other 49er. Since joining the team in 1985, he has led the NFL four times in receiving yards.

Rice, the 49ers' legendary receiver, said that he wasn't getting enough passes. "I miss Joe out there," he told a reporter.[2] The best he could say about Young was, "He's a great *running* quarterback."[3] That remark irritated Young. "Call me a quarterback," he said, "not a running quarterback."[4] He felt he had proven that he was a good passer.

Young still refused to say anything bad about Montana, Rice, or any of his other teammates. When he got tired of the complaints about his playing, he just didn't say anything. It was obvious that he wasn't having much fun being the starting quarterback. "I'd like him to enjoy it a little more," said Mike Holmgren, San Francisco's defensive coordinator. "Hey," Young answered, "everybody wants me to laugh. I'm thinking, 'Hey, I gotta work.'"[5]

In a game with Los Angeles, the Rams had a 10–3 lead with only forty-one seconds left in the first half. Then Young started clicking. It took him only twenty-three seconds to move the ball into the end zone, the last 12 yards on a pass to John Taylor. In the second half, the 49er offense kept rolling as Rice caught a 62-yard scoring pass. Young connected on 21 of 31 passes for 288 yards. After the game, he finally appeared to be enjoying himself. "That felt good," he said. "It was my team this week and that's good enough for me."[6]

Forty-niner legend Jerry Rice wanted Steve to throw the ball to him more often. Rice and Joe Montana had been a lethal combination.

Montana had hoped to be ready for the fifth game of the season, but his elbow still hadn't healed, so Young was back on the field for a disappointing 12–6 loss to the Los Angeles Raiders. Then the 49er defense fell apart in a 39–34 defeat at the hands of the Atlanta Falcons. The 49er fans could hardly believe it. Their team had a 3–4 record. Instead of planning for the Super Bowl, they were hoping just to finish the season with a winning record. Of course, the man who got most of the blame was Young.

Their next opponents were the surprising Detroit Lions. Led by running back Barry Sanders, they had won five games in a row after losing their opener to the Washington Redskins. The Lions looked forward to the chance to knock off the 49ers. "We're not going to get any real respect until we can beat the San Franciscos and Washingtons," said Detroit quarterback Rodney Peete.[7] He couldn't wait to work against the 49er defense that had given up 39 points to the Falcons.

Against the Lions, the 49ers held firm. Detroit only got a field goal. During most of the game, San Francisco had the ball, and Young was unstoppable. "It seemed like we were on the field all the time," said Dennis Gibson, a Detroit linebacker.[8] The 49ers never had to punt. Young missed only 2 of 20

Second-string quarterback Steve Young was named NFC Offensive Player of the Month for October 1991.

FACT

Bones form the body's skeleton, but muscles actually move the body. Ligaments are bands of tissue that hold bones together. Tendons are the cords that connect muscles to bones. Athletic injuries usually involve twisted or torn muscles, ligaments, or tendons. The tissues bleed, causing swelling and discolored skin. If the tear is severe, surgery might be required.

passes. He threw for a pair of touchdowns—a 2-yarder to Rice, and one for 22 yards to Mike Sherrard. He also picked up 40 more yards in 7 carries. That earned him honors as NFC Offensive Player of the Week. No other San Francisco quarterback—not even Montana—had ever completed 90 percent of his passes.

After the 49ers whipped the Philadelphia Eagles, 23–7, Young was named NFC Offensive Player of the Month. During October, he completed 68.5 percent of his passes, totaling 681 yards and 5 touchdowns.

Against Atlanta, he hit Taylor with a 97-yard scoring pass, another San Francisco record. Then, just before the end of the first half, he twisted his left knee. He had pulled a ligament and had to sit out the rest of the game. With Steve Bono, the third-string quarterback, on the field, the 49ers lost, 17–14.

Young wouldn't be able to play for three weeks. San Francisco lost to New Orleans, 10–3, but then Bono got hot, and the team beat the Phoenix Cardinals, 14–10, and the Rams, 33–10.

Young was ready for action the next week, but by then he had lost the starting job. Coach George Seifert decided that Bono had earned the right to stay on the field. With Young dressed but standing on the sidelines, the 49ers beat the Saints, 38–24, and the Seattle Seahawks, 24–22.

Riding the bench was an uncomfortable but familiar spot for Young. It didn't really matter that instead of watching Montana, he was watching Bono. After four years of waiting, he finally had the starting job because of an injury, only to lose it when he was injured himself.

Then, against the Kansas City Chiefs, Bono became the third San Francisco signal-caller in 1991 to suffer an injury; he hurt his knee in the third quarter. Suddenly Young was back on the field, completing 2 of 4 passes as the 49ers took a 28–14 victory.

Since the 49ers had not qualified for the playoffs, their last game would be the regular-season finale against the Bears. Young decided to stop letting the struggle for a starting job get him upset. "I came back for the last game of the 1991 season much more at peace with myself about everything," he said. "I knew I had to relax more and let everything come together. I decided I just had to be me and play ball."[9]

Seifert was pleased with Young's new attitude. "Before that game, Steve had played very well, but many times he seemed to be struggling, almost as if he were fighting with himself. I told him to just move the club and not worry about how he had to do it. I said, 'You have God-given abilities. Just take advantage of them.'"[10]

Young's new attitude seemed to work. He threw for 3 touchdowns with 21 completions out of 32 passes. He felt confident enough to pick up 63 yards and a touchdown running the ball. He was now sure of himself, and of his ability to lead the team. "I used to try to do everything possible all at once, sometimes on every play," he said. "After I got hurt, I realized it was my job to orchestrate the offense, not play every instrument."[11]

Many San Francisco fans didn't notice Young's new attitude and paid no attention to his fine statistics. Remembering that for the first time in nine years their team had failed to make the playoffs, they figured it would have been different if Montana had been able to play.

Everybody expected Joe to be back for the 1992 season. Young hoped that his fine play had earned him a chance to keep the job. After all, when he had been injured, Bono became the starter, a position Bono didn't lose until he himself was injured. While Young was wondering if he'd be San Francisco's number-one quarterback, the team was trying to get rid of him.

Chapter 8

Not Wanted

After the 1991 season, the San Francisco 49ers had three of the best quarterbacks in football. Joe Montana was healing, and he was itching to get back into action; Steve Young had just had the best year of his professional career; and Steve Bono had taken over and led the team well when the other two men were injured. The 49ers were beginning to wonder if three fine quarterbacks were one too many.

"The coaches said Joe was throwing better than he had in years," said Carmen Policy, team president. "And the prospect of Steve Young being an unhappy camper would have been a distraction to the team."[1] He figured that Montana would be ready to start, and with Bono on the bench, why keep Young? After being a starter for most of a

Waiting for his chance to become starting quarterback matured Steve Young. By the end of the 1991 season, he had developed a new, confident attitude.

season, Young probably wouldn't be satisfied to ride the bench. Why not trade him to another team and pick up some players or draft choices the team could use?

No other team wanted Young, however. At least they wouldn't give up enough to get him. Nobody believed that he was superstar material; he was just a second-string quarterback who'd had a few lucky games. When the 49ers couldn't make any deals for Young, they were stuck with him.

Then the doctors told the team that Montana's elbow still wasn't completely healed. The 49ers were down to just two quarterbacks. Coach George Seifert decided to let Young and Bono compete for the job. After watching them both in preseason exhibition games, he gave the starting job to Young.

He didn't last long. On only the fifth play of the opener against the New York Giants, he suffered another concussion. He had to come out of the game, and Bono took over. San Francisco won, 31–14, but Young spent most of the game watching.

He was back on the field the next week against the Buffalo Bills, and he threw for a spectacular total of 449 yards and 3 touchdowns. Still, the Bills won, 34–31.

Young got the team back on track with consistently strong passing and occasional runs, leading

FACT

A concussion occurs when the brain bounces against the inside of the skull, which sometimes happens when the head is bumped. Football players wear helmets to protect them against head injuries, but concussions still occur. Sometimes the player is knocked unconscious or forgets where he is. If the concussion is not too severe, the player can return to the game.

them to victories over the New York Jets, New Orleans Saints, Los Angeles Rams, New England Patriots, and Atlanta Falcons.

Despite the team's success, many fans still waited anxiously for Montana's return. Reporters watching him practice wondered when he'd be ready to play again. "Last week," he said.[2] The doctors told him to wait.

"Joe was one of the greatest who ever played and now he's watching me," Young said. "There's a part of me that says, 'Jeez, Joe, I want to play well. What do you think?'"[3]

Young really got a chance to show his stuff on November 15. New Orleans surprised the 49ers by taking a 20–7 lead early in the fourth quarter. It was time to get the team moving. To catch the Saints off guard, he decided to concentrate on throwing to his tight ends. He figured that the secondary would be concentrating on Rice.

With twelve minutes to go, Young hit Brent Jones for 20 yards. But his ribs were bruised in a crushing tackle and he had to leave the game. No problem; the next two passes went to his replacement, Jamie Williams. Young planned to keep going to Williams, but then Jones ran back onto the field. His ribs hurt every time he breathed, but he was ready to gut it out and finish the game. As Jones cut

Young goes back for a long one.

across the middle, Young connected with a beautiful 12-yard touchdown pass. The Saints' lead had shrunk to 20–14.

Then, with four minutes to go, the 49ers took over the ball again at their 26-yard line. With the Candlestick Park crowd screaming encouragement, Young called the plays and slowly moved the ball downfield. Twice he was faced with tough third-down plays, and twice he turned to Jerry Rice, who made nice catches and earned a pair of first downs.

Then quickly it was third down again. Young was sure that the Saints expected him to go to Rice this time, too, so he told the team he was going to take the ball. "The whole huddle just kind of went, 'Jeez, here we go again,'" he said. "'The quarterback's gonna run the ball. Watch out.'"[4] They were afraid he was going back to his old habit of running himself whenever the situation was tough, but it was a great call. He ran for the sideline and got the first down.

Tailback Ricky Watters took the ball twice, putting the 49ers at the 8-yard line. Young told Jones to get ready for another pass. The tight end was still having trouble breathing, but he was anxious to make another reception. It was the same play that had worked before, and Jones was wide open in the end zone when Young threw him the ball.

Touchdown! Jones spiked the ball. He didn't care if his ribs hurt. The kick gave San Francisco a 21–20 victory.

The crowd cheered wildly for Young and the come-from-behind victory. For a while at least, it seemed as though they weren't waiting anxiously for Montana's return. The players seemed satisfied with their quarterback, too. "That last drive," said guard Guy McIntyre, "he was just as calm as Joe ever was."[5]

The win over New Orleans was part of an eight-game winning streak that ended the regular season. Young went almost all the way. Montana wasn't back on the roster until the second to last game, and he didn't play until the last half of the finale. "It's been a while so I figured I'd be rusty," Montana said. "I just tried to tell myself not to be overcautious. I just didn't want to make a big mistake."[6]

Montana threw a pair of touchdowns and completed 15 of 16 passes as San Francisco beat Detroit, 24–6. It was a good performance, especially for a man who hadn't played in two years, but the starting job, for a while at least, still belonged to Young. In fact, Seifert said he wasn't sure whether Bono or Montana would be the backup quarterback in the playoffs.

The 49ers were counting on Young to take them

In 1992, Steve Young was named the NFL's Most
Valuable Player.

to the Super Bowl. "It's your team," the coach told him. "It's your football."[7] After leading the league with 25 touchdown passes and a 66.7 completion percentage, Young earned the NFL's Most Valuable Player honors. *Sports Illustrated* and *The Sporting News* named him Player of the Year. His teammates voted him the Len Eshmont Award as the team's most inspirational and courageous player. Even Rice had good things to say about Young. "He's had an MVP year, no doubt about it. He has an attitude now, you can just look at him whenever he takes the field, he's got confidence in himself."[8]

A week of rain had turned Candlestick Park into a bowl of mud for the first playoff game with the Washington Redskins. It was so sloppy that everybody had trouble hanging on to the ball. Each team had four turnovers.

Young was able to complete a pair of first-half scoring passes—a 5-yarder to John Taylor, and another for 16 to Brent Jones. At the half, San Francisco led, 17–3. Then he fumbled twice, leading to a field goal and a touchdown by Washington. All of a sudden the score was 17–13. Seifert told Montana to warm up. Off came the jacket, and he began tossing the ball on the sidelines. Young knew that one more mistake might send him to the bench.

He took the 49ers on a slow but steady drive that

FACT

The San Francisco 49ers and the Dallas Cowboys have been great rivals since their first game in 1960. In their twenty-three meetings, each team has won eleven times, and there has been one tie. During the decade between 1981 and 1990, when the 49ers took four Super Bowls, they won all six games against the Cowboys.

ate up seven minutes. Mike Cofer finished it up with a field goal. That made the final score 20–13. Montana never made it onto the field. Young said he wasn't bothered by Montana's warm-up tosses: "I'm here now and this is my job."[9]

Young opened the NFC championship game against the Cowboys with a 63-yard touchdown pass to Rice, but the score was nullified by a holding penalty. That was the sort of action he was talking about when he said later, "There were so many plays that turned the game their way."[10]

When Alan Grant fumbled on a punt return, Dallas took the ball and marched downfield for a field goal. When Watters lost the ball running a sweep, the Cowboys came back with a 4-yard touchdown run by Emmitt Smith. At the half, it was tied, 10–10.

Then Darryl Johnston put Dallas ahead with a 3-yard TD run. After a Cofer field goal tightened the score to 17–13, the Cowboys' Troy Aikman hit Smith with a swing pass from 16 yards out that made it 24–13.

San Francisco wasn't finished yet. Midway through the fourth quarter, Young got them moving from their own 7. He knew that if he could get a quick score, there would still be time to take the lead. With 4:22 remaining on the clock, he flipped

Troy Aikman is the star quarterback of the Dallas Cowboys. Aikman and Young, two of today's greatest quarterbacks, both wear No. 8.

Rice a 5-yard touchdown. The 49ers trailed, 24–20. Rice jumped up on the bench to lead the Candlestick Park crowd in cheers. Many of them could smell another come-from-behind victory.

As soon as the Cowboys got the ball, Aikman tossed a short pass to Alvin Harper, who took off for 70 yards. Rice climbed off the bench, and the San Francisco fans quieted. Three plays later, Aikman hit Kelvin Martin for 6 yards and the final score. Dallas won, 30–20.

Joe Montana walked quietly off the field and disappeared before reporters made their way into the locker room. He and many of the fans wondered if he had played his last game for the 49ers.[11] Steve Young patiently answered questions, confident that his future was secure in San Francisco.

They were both in for some surprises.

Chapter 9

Starting Quarterback

Now that his elbow had healed, Joe Montana said that he was too old to sit on the bench. "It's always tough when you sit and watch when you know you can still play," he said. "Anyone who isn't anxious to get out on the field doesn't deserve to be out there in the first place."[1] Was he still tough enough to play in the NFL? "People who have seen me throw know that I'm no different than before, just a little older."[2]

He wanted the San Francisco 49ers' starting quarterback's slot that had been his for a decade, but the team said the job belonged to Young. Montana would be the number two quarterback; the 49ers weren't big enough for two great quarterbacks. "It would have been very chaotic if both of us had stayed," he said later. "It would have been a very difficult situation. Everybody would have wanted to know who's going to start this game or that."[3] If he couldn't start in San Francisco, Montana wanted to go somewhere else.

In the spring of 1993, he talked with several other teams. The Kansas City Chiefs said that they wanted him; they would be willing to make a trade with San Francisco. When Montana asked the 49ers to approve the trade, however, the team's management panicked. What would the fans say if they gave Montana away? How could they trade the superstar who had brought them four Super Bowl championships? Coach George Seifert forgot his promise to Young. He announced that if Montana stayed in San Francisco, he would be the 49ers' "designated starter" for the 1993 season.[4]

Montana couldn't believe Seifert's offer. How could the team completely change its mind? How would Young feel? What if the coach changed his mind again? Montana decided it was time to leave. He asked the 49ers again to trade him to the Chiefs.

How did the NFL's Most Valuable Player feel when his coach tried to give away his job? "Shocked?" he asked. "Yeah, absolutely."[5] Seifert hadn't even called to tell him about the team's change in plans. Young had found out about it by watching television, but he tried not to let it upset

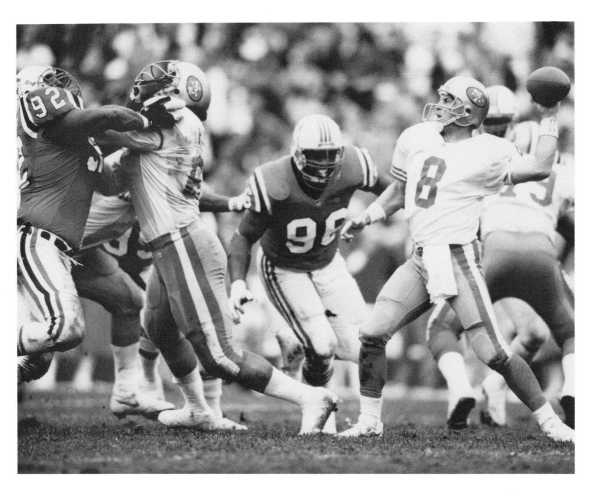

With great passing, Young led the 49ers to a victory over the New England Patriots.

him. "My head was in the books," he said.[6] Once again he was back in Provo taking law classes at Brigham Young University. Instead of getting mad about the attempted deal with Montana, he concentrated on studying for finals.

Finally, Montana got his way; the 49ers traded him to the Chiefs. Young was relieved, but, he said, "I'm glad it was April and I had a few days to let it fall out. As you look through my career, I've learned to take a deep breath and sleep on it."[7] He refused to say anything bad about the team or Montana. "I wish the best for him. Can you imagine? Two years ago he couldn't throw the ball. Now he's going to come back and play."[8]

Three months later, Young signed a big contract with San Francisco that helped him forget the treatment he had received in the spring. It only took a day of negotiating between his agent, Leigh Steinberg, and the team. Young signed a five-year, $26.5-million deal. He would earn $5.3 million a year, more than $330,000 for every regular season game.

Now that the team was all his, he had some advice for 49er fans: "Some people also sense they have to choose between me and Joe. I never felt they had to choose. I'd urge everyone to have the attitude, 'Go, 49ers.'"[9]

He promised them a good season: "Jerry Rice

FACT

It's not easy to become an attorney. First, prospective lawyers have to earn bachelor degrees from a college. If their grades are high enough, they can then be accepted into a law school. It usually takes three years of full-time study to earn a law degree. It took Steve Young longer to get through law school, because he could only take classes in the spring, when he wasn't playing football.

and I were working better together as the [1992] season went on, and we should be smoother this year. . . . That's the kind of thing we'll be looking for."[10]

What Young wasn't looking for was another injury. In a preseason game, he slammed his throwing hand on the helmet of a Los Angeles Raider, breaking his thumb. That didn't stop him from practicing, but for three weeks, he had to use a sponge football. He told Seifert that the injury wouldn't prevent him from starting the regular season. "I could probably go out and throw all day as long as I don't do anything stupid," he said. "I mean, hitting my hand on a helmet would be a bad deal, and I won't get in any fights, either."[11]

As he warmed up for the opener against the Pittsburgh Steelers, the thumb started to swell. "I'm sure he's still sore and it's bothering him," said tight end Brent Jones, "but Steve won't admit it."[12] It bothered Young enough that he asked his center, Jesse Sapolu, to snap the ball into his right hand, instead of his left.

In the first half, Young hit Rice with a pair of touchdown passes, and San Francisco led, 17–3. Then the Steelers came back with a Barry Foster touchdown and another Gary Anderson field goal, to cut the lead to 17–13.

Young didn't want to watch the victory slip away. The 49ers took the ball at their own 20-yard line and started moving. Along the way, Young's passing was perfect—5 for 5, for 55 yards. He ended the drive with a 5-yard TD toss to Jones, and San Francisco won, 24–13. "We're celebrating this one," he said. "I haven't played in a month, they've got a great defense . . . and we score seventeen straight points. . . . I'm proud of this one."[13]

After a disappointing loss to Cleveland, the 49ers trailed Atlanta, 20–16, in the third quarter, but a 70-yard San Francisco drive made it 23–20 when Young handed off to Ricky Watters, who jumped into the end zone from the two. Then the quarterback completed his third TD pass of the game, a 6-yarder to Nate Singleton. The 49ers won, 37–30.

Steve completed 22 of 30 passes (73.3 percent), but San Francisco lost to New Orleans, 16–13. Playing against Minnesota, Young suffered a slight concussion, but he kept going. He hit on 17 of 24 passes for 224 yards, on the way to a 38–19 victory.

Then came a 26–17 loss to Dallas and a 28–14 win over Phoenix. Young threw for 245 yards as the 49ers raised their record to 5–3 by beating the Los Angeles Rams, 40–17.

The next game was Young's first starting assignment at Tampa Bay since the Buccaneers had traded

With Ricky Watters, the 49ers developed an excellent running game to complement their famous passing game.

him. He and Rice had an incredible day. They teamed up for 7 completions, 146 yards, and 4 touchdowns. The Bucs fell, 45–21.

Young and Rice were still hot as the 49ers took their fourth in a row, a 42–7 win over the Saints. The duo got 2 more touchdowns. "A lot of people were counting us out, so it feels good to come out and play a game like that," Rice said. "I think we've matured a lot and we're starting to peak at the right time."[14] The playoffs were less than two months away.

In Los Angeles, the 49ers buried the Rams, 35–10, as Young's passing accounted for 462 yards, the best single-game total of his NFL career. He completed 26 of 32 (81.3 percent), and threw for 4 touchdowns. That performance helped earn him NFC Offensive Player of the Month honors for November. In four games that month, he passed for 978 yards and 4 touchdowns.

After defeating Cincinnati, 21–8, and losing to Atlanta, 27–24, San Francisco had to face the Detroit Lions on December 19. On the 49ers' third play, Young hit John Taylor with a 68-yard TD pass. As soon as they got the ball again, he connected with Sanjay Beach for 20 yards and a score. The Lions answered with a field goal, and San Francisco had the ball at the 20. Young flung a long pass to Rice, but Detroit's Kevin Scott got his hands on the ball, and it looked like he had an interception. Then Rice yanked the ball out of his hands, and took off for a touchdown. After that, the Lions never had a chance, and they lost, 55–17.

In that game, Steve's 354 passing yards gave him 3,680 for the season, his best ever. His 4 TD passes raised his season total to 27, and he still had two regular season games to go. The 49ers lost both of them, 25–7 to Houston and 37–34 to Philadelphia, but they had already qualified for the playoffs. Many of the quarterbacking duties in those two games were handled by Steve Bono, so Young could rest. Young's final season totals, 4,023 yards passing and 29 touchdowns, made him the first 49er quarterback to throw more than four thousand yards in a season.

His postseason goal was very clear: "Respect is something you get from other players in the league and you get that by playing. . . . You can take yourself to a level above and you do that by going to the Super Bowl."[15] All the 49ers had to do was win two playoff games.

In the first quarter against the New York Giants, Steve engineered an 80-yard drive that ended in Watters's one-yard plunge. On the next possession, he took them close enough for a field goal. After Tim

McDonald picked off a New York pass, the 49ers were off and running again. Soon Watters had popped into the end zone from the one.

The Giants couldn't believe what Young and his team were doing to them. "It was like a track meet," said Coach Dan Reeves. "They looked like they were on some fast ponies and we were on some slow mules."[16] Even in the huddle, some of the players were talking about the 49ers. "Some of the guys were saying, 'Man, these guys are good,'" said New York's Greg Jackson. "I was so mad I couldn't believe it. . . . They were shell-shocked, scared."[17]

Young finished with 17 completions out of 22 passes (77.3 percent) for 226 yards as San Francisco rolled to an overwhelming 44–3 triumph. Now only one team stood between the 49ers and the Super Bowl—the Dallas Cowboys.

Emmitt Smith put the Cowboys on the scoreboard first with a 5-yard run in the first quarter, but the 49ers came right back when a Young-Tom Rathman pass was good for 7 yards and a touchdown.

After Darryl Johnston's 4-yard scoring run, San Francisco tried to tie the game again, but this time Steve's pass was intercepted at the 49er 38 by Thomas Everett, who ran it back to the 24. Four plays later, Troy Aikman hit Smith for 11 yards and another score. When Young couldn't move his team, the 49ers had to punt. Minutes later a 19-yard Aikman pass found Jay Novacek in the end zone. Dallas led at the half, 28–7.

San Francisco wasn't finished yet. Young handed the ball to Watters, who got a 4-yard scoring run midway through the third quarter. If they could keep Dallas from moving the ball, they still had a chance to win. By then, Aikman was injured and on the bench. With Bernie Kosar taking his place, the Cowboys had a third-down-and-nine situation from their own 19. The 49er defense closed in on Kosar, but he flipped a 12-yarder to Michael Irvin for the first down. Four plays later, Alvin Harper caught a Kosar pass for 42 yards and a touchdown. It was 35–14, and the 49ers were finished.

Young scored on a one-yard plunge in the last quarter, and the final score was 38–21. Despite being sacked 4 times by the tough Dallas pass rush, he had completed 27 of 45 passes (60 percent), but he had thrown a crucial interception and had been unable to come up with enough big plays. The season was over, and the 49ers would have to wait at least another year for a shot at the Super Bowl.

Chapter 10

The Star

On September 11, 1994, Steve Young and Joe Montana faced each other. For the first time since the big trade, the San Francisco 49ers would be playing the Kansas City Chiefs.

"There was a lot of emotion going into this game for both teams," Montana said. "But if you're a competitor, you like the challenge of trying to beat a team you once played for."[1] Young kept pointing out that the game was more than just a match between two quarterbacks; it was a battle between two fine teams.

Young knew he still had to prove himself. He was San Francisco's starting quarterback, but many 49er fans missed Montana. With Young starting, the team had been knocked out of the playoffs two years in a row by the Dallas Cowboys. Would it

When it was announced that Young would become the starting
quarterback, Montana shopped around for another team. He
was picked up by the Kansas City Chiefs. That season, Montana
led the Chiefs to the playoffs.

have been different with Montana running the offense?

In the game against Kansas City, the 49ers were in trouble right from the start. Three of their starting offensive linemen were out with injuries, which meant that Young would be protected by an inexperienced line. San Francisco was still able to take a 14–7 lead.

In the second quarter, deep in his own territory, Young couldn't get away from linebacker Derrick Thomas, who knocked him down in the end zone. Then Montana took over, finally lobbing an 8-yard scoring pass to Keith Cash that put the Chiefs ahead for good.

With four minutes left and trailing 24–17, Young was moving the 49ers once again. He threw a strike to John Taylor at midfield, but the Chiefs' George Jamison ripped it from his grasp.

"You could say I took a pretty healthy beating," Young said. He had to dodge charging Chiefs all night, and he was sacked 4 times. "But I knew this was going to be a hard-hitting game. That's how I kept myself focused throughout all the hype this week. While everyone else focused on me against Joe, I knew it was going to be me against a very good Kansas City defense."[2]

Young sat on the bench watching Montana run

Steve signals to the sideline.

out the clock. He was exhausted and wiped out. Hoping that nobody would notice, he turned away from the action and vomited over and over onto the turf. Teammate Steve Wallace threw his arm around his friend and waited for the game to end. "He didn't have anything left," Wallace said.[3] Young agreed. "I don't think I could've gone another series. The idea is that I'd be disappointed if I didn't leave it all on the field."[4]

When it was over, Young walked over to Montana and congratulated him. Back in the locker room, he patiently answered reporters' questions. He didn't complain or offer excuses. Instead, he told them that Joe was "the master."[5]

On November 13, 1994, the Super Bowl champion Cowboys came to Candlestick Park. The 49ers hadn't beaten them in four years. Young couldn't beat Montana and the Chiefs. Could he lead San Francisco to a win over Dallas?

Early in the first quarter, Young faked a handoff to running back Ricky Watters, then ran around left end himself. The Cowboys hadn't expected him to act like a running back, and they didn't catch him until he'd gone 25 yards. Then for the rest of the day, they had to be careful rushing Young since they didn't want him to slip away again.

After Emmitt Smith's 4-yard touchdown run

gave Dallas an early lead, Young tied the game with a one-yard dive. The score was 7–7, but Steve and the 49ers had only gained 98 yards in the first half to 237 for the Cowboys. He had to get the offense moving if he wanted to finally beat Dallas.

Maybe he remembered what his great receiver Jerry Rice had said about the Cowboys a few days before the game: "It's like you're going to school, and you've got this bully who's taking your lunch money every day. What are you going to do? Eventually you take a stand."[6] Rice and all the 49ers were tired of the Cowboys taking their "lunch money."

Late in the third quarter, from his own 43, Young heaved a long pass that hit Rice at the 17. San Francisco's super receiver broke a tackle and raced into the end zone. The 49ers led, 14–7.

After the San Francisco defense held tight, Young and the offense took over at their 13. With 2:32 left, he connected with receiver Brent Jones for a 13-yard scoring pass. Young, normally a quiet, calm player, leaped into the air, waving his arms. Then he raced into the end zone to hug Jones. After a late Cowboys touchdown, San Francisco won, 21–14.

The 49ers finished the regular season with a 13–3 record. Steve threw for 35 touchdowns and 3,969 yards. He completed 70.3 percent of his passes, better than any of Montana's totals. He was named the league's Most Valuable Player.

In the first game of the playoffs, San Francisco blasted the Chicago Bears, 44–15. Young was confident: "I feel like I'm in total control. This offense has the answers to anything anybody does defensively."[7]

Then, for the third year in a row, the 49ers met Dallas in the conference title game. Once again, Young and his teammates seemed angry about having their "lunch money" stolen. They jumped to a 21–0 first-quarter lead, then hung on to win, 38–28. Finally, Young had beaten the Cowboys in the playoffs and earned a spot for his team in the Super Bowl.

Young still had to prove he could win the biggest game of them all. Super Bowl XXIX was the greatest game of his career. He threw for 6 touchdowns, as San Francisco demolished San Diego, 49–26.

Steve Young knows that there is more to life than football. In 1993, he finished law school at Brigham Young University. When his sports career is over, he plans to be an attorney. "People are in trouble," he said. "This huge, ugly system faces them and you're the only way to get people through the maze."[8] He wants to help people who need a break.

Despite making more than $5 million a year, he doesn't live in a fancy house or drive expensive

The 49ers blasted the Chargers in Super Bowl XXIX.

FACT

The Navajo tribes lived in the Southwest until they were defeated by United States soldiers in the 1860s. The survivors were forced to walk more than three hundred miles to Fort Sumner, New Mexico. Thousands of them died on this Long Walk. Today, one hundred thousand Navajos live on a reservation that covers parts of Utah, Arizona, and New Mexico.

sports cars. His sister, Melissa Massey, says he lives in "an old pioneer house. Two tiny bedrooms. For a long time it didn't have a kitchen, and didn't have a stove. It was a condemned house, and he fixed it up a little bit. So it's not condemned anymore." His car is just as bad. "He has this really old convertible. It's really ugly."[9]

When he won a car for being named the Super Bowl Most Valuable Player, he seemed almost embarrassed. "I'm not sure what I'm going to do with a new car," he said. "I'm panicked about the whole thing. I think what I'll do is just take it out and scratch it up and beat on it a little bit and then I'll feel much better about it."[10]

Steve Young doesn't care about what his sister—or anybody else—thinks about his house or his car. "The only fun I have with money is to be able to spread it around and do some fun things for people."[11] Without a lot of fuss, each time the 49ers win, he donates $2,500 to San Francisco's public high school sports program.

He has also donated money and time to various causes benefiting Navajos living in four western states. He gives talks at reservations and arranges for scholarships that have sent hundreds of Native Americans to college. Russian immigrants living in Utah have also benefited from his generosity, and he set up the Forever Young Foundation to distribute money to charities.

Of course, Steve Young is earning money a lot faster than he's spending it—or giving it away. Besides his earnings from the 49ers, he's also now making millions from endorsements. Three months after the 1995 Super Bowl, he and Rice signed multimillion dollar deals with All Sport Body Quencher™, a sports drink. "Jerry Rice and Steve Young are giants—on and off the football field," said the drink's marketing director.[12] The two stars hoped to make All Sport™ as popular as Gatorade™, the beverage promoted by Michael Jordan.

Steve isn't famous just for his advertising or for his generosity. He's famous because he's one of the greatest quarterbacks ever to play professional football. He's already set records and made incredible plays, and he hopes that he still has a few great seasons left.

As he pointed out as he celebrated after Super Bowl XXIX, "I'll always remember this as my best effort, but I hope there's more to come."[13]

From the bench to the record books, Steve Young has defied his critics and become the NFL's leading quarterback.

Notes by Chapter

Chapter 1

1. Mike Lopresti, Gannett News Service column, January 28, 1995.

2. Rich Telander, "Superb!," *Sports Illustrated,* vol. 82, no. 5, February 6, 1995, p. 30.

3. Bill Berkrot, Reuter's dispatch, Miami, January 30, 1995.

4. Ibid.

5. Erik Brady, "MVP Award Confirms Young as Superhero," *USA Today,* January 30, 1995, p. 1C.

6. Ibid.

7. Berkrot.

Chapter 2

1. Richard J. Brenner, *Troy Aikman/Steve Young* (Syosset, N.Y.: East End Publishing, 1994), p. 53.

2. Judith Graham, ed., "Steve Young," *Current Biography,* (October 1993), vol. 54, no. 10, p. 55.

3. Mike Lopresti, Gannett News Service column, January 22, 1995.

4. Walter Roessing, "Steve Young: The Mad Scrambler," *Boys' Life,* December 1993, p. 67.

5. Brenner, p. 53.

6. Ibid., p. 54.

7. Roessing, p. 67.

8. Brenner, p. 54.

9. Ibid.

10. Ibid., p. 57.

Chapter 3

1. Rick Telander, "Superb!" *Sports Illustrated,* vol. 82, no. 5, February 6, 1995, p. 38.

2. Judith Graham, ed., "Steve Young," *Current Biography,* (October 1993), vol. 54, no. 10, p. 55.

3. Mike Lopresti, Gannett News Service column, January 22, 1995.

4. Richard J. Brenner, *Troy Aikman/Steve Young* (Syosset, N.Y.: East End Publishing, 1994), p. 58.

5. Ibid., p. 59.

6. Ibid., p. 61.

7. "Steve Young NCAA Records," Brigham Young University Sports Information Office.

Chapter 4

1. Peter King, "Young and the Restless," *Sports Illustrated*, vol. 78, no. 21, May 31, 1993, p. 69.

2. Ibid., p. 70.

3. Ibid., p. 73.

4. Ibid.

5. Ibid.

Chapter 5

1. Ron Juanso, *San Francisco 49ers 1993 Official Yearbook* (San Francisco: Woodford Publishing, 1993), p. 17.

2. Peter King, "Young and the Restless," *Sports Illustrated*, vol. 78, no. 21, May 31, 1993, p. 74.

3. Mark Fainaru, "Steve Young Q & A," *Sport*, vol. 84, no. 8, August 1993, p. 37.

4. King, p. 74.

5. Ibid.

6. Fainaru, p. 33.

Chapter 6

1. Richard J. Brenner, *Troy Aikman/Steve Young* (Syosset, N.Y.: East End Publishing, 1994), p. 69.

2. Bill Walsh and Glenn Dickey, *Building a Champion* (New York: St. Martin's Press, 1990), p. 230.

3. Mike Lopresti, Gannett News Service column, January 28, 1995.

4. Walsh and Dickey, p. 236.

5. Walter Roessing, "Steve Young: The Mad Scrambler," *Boys' Life*, December 1993, p. 23.

6. Ibid.

7. Peter King, "Young and the Restless," *Sports Illustrated,* vol. 78, no. 21, May 31, 1993, p. 76.

8. Rick Reilly, "The Young 49ers," *Sports Illustrated,* vol. 75, no. 14, September 30, 1991, p. 26.

9. Mark Fainaru, "Steve Young Q & A," *Sport,* vol. 84, no. 8, August 1993, p. 35.

10. King, p. 77.

11. Brenner, p. 70.

12. Ibid.

Chapter 7

1. Peter King, "Young and the Restless," *Sports Illustrated,* vol. 78, no. 21, May 31, 1993, p. 77.

2. Rick Reilly, "The Young 49ers," *Sports Illustrated,* vol. 75, no. 14, September 30, 1991, p. 26.

3. Richard J. Brenner, *Troy Aikman/Steve Young* (Syosset, N.Y.: East End Publishing, 1994), p. 72.

4. King, p. 76.

5. Reilly, p. 26.

6. Ibid., p. 31.

7. Associated Press dispatch, San Francisco, October 20, 1991.

8. Ibid.

9. Judith Graham, ed., "Steve Young," *Current Biography,* (October 1993), vol. 54, no. 10, p. 56.

10. Ibid.

11. Ibid.

Chapter 8

1. Peter King, "Young and the Restless," *Sports Illustrated,* vol. 78, no. 21, May 31, 1993, p. 76.

2. Rick Reilly, "He Did It His Way," *Sports Illustrated,* vol. 77, no. 22, November 23, 1992, p. 30.

3. Ibid., p. 32.

4. Ibid., p. 33.

5. Ibid.

6. Associated Press dispatch, San Francisco, December 28, 1992.

7. Dave Anderson, "Montana's Stand-In Scenario," *The New York Times,* January 17, 1993, sec. 8, p. 1.

8. Richard J. Brenner, *Troy Aikman/Steve Young* (Syosset, N.Y.: East End Publishing, 1994), p. 77.

9. Ibid., p. 78.

10. Associated Press dispatch, San Francisco, January 17, 1993.

11. Ibid.

Chapter 9

1. Dave Anderson, "Montana's Stand-In Scenario," *The New York Times,* January 17, 1993, sec. 8, p. 1.

2. Timothy W. Smith, "Complete: Young Gets 5-Year Deal," *The New York Times,* July 16, 1993, p. B12.

3. Ibid.

4. Tom Friend, "Young Hit Books, Not Ceiling, During His Demotion," *The New York Times,* April 23, 1993, p. B15.

5. Ibid.

6. Ibid.

7. Ibid.

8. Timothy W. Smith, "An Upbeat Young Gets Out of Montana's Shadow," *The New York Times,* May 27, 1993, p. B14.

9. Friend, p. B15.

10. Judith Graham, ed., "Steve Young," *Current Biography,* (October 1993), vol. 54, no. 10, p. 57.

11. Timothy W. Smith, "Ailing Young Fights Against a Big Shadow," *The New York Times,* August 27, 1993, p. B13.

12. Associated Press dispatch, Pittsburgh, September 5, 1993.

13. Ibid.

14. Associated Press dispatch, San Francisco, November 22, 1993.

15. Mike Freeman, "As Young Prepares for Giants, There Remains a Lot to Prove," *The New York Times,* January 13, 1994, p. B9.

16. Mike Freeman, "Giants' Dream Season Ends in a Million Pieces," *The New York Times,* January 16, 1994, sec. 8, p. 3.

17. Ibid., p. 1.

Chapter 10

1. Drew Sharp, "Montana Beats 49ers as Mates Beat on Young," *Detroit Free Press,* September 12, 1994, p. C3.

2. Ibid.

3. Rick Telander, "Superb!," *Sports Illustrated,* vol. 82, no. 5, February 6, 1995, p. 22.

4. Ibid., p. 26.

5. Sharp, p. C3.

6. Rick Telander, "Stuffed!," *Sports Illustrated,* vol. 81, no. 21, November 21, 1994, p. 25.

7. Rick Telander and Peter King, "Destroyers," *Sports Illustrated,* vol. 82, no. 2, January 16, 1995, p. 18.

8. Richard J. Brenner, *Troy Aikman/Steve Young* (Syosset, N.Y.: East End Publishing, 1994), p. 83.

9. Mike Lopresti, Gannett News Service column, January 22, 1995.

10. Bill Berkrot, "Long, Strange Trip for Super Bowl MVP Steve Young," Reuter's dispatch, Miami, January 30, 1995.

11. Brenner, p. 83.

12. PR Newswire dispatch, Somers, N.Y., April 20, 1995.

13. Larry Weisman, "Right Now, We Are the Very Best," *USA Today,* January 30, 1995.

Career Statistics

Year	Team	ATT	Comp	Yards	%	TD	Int
1984	L.A. Express	310	179	2,361	57.7	10	9
1985	L.A. Express	250	137	1,741	54.8	6	13
USFL Totals		560	316	4,102	56.4	16	22

Year	Team	ATT	Comp	Yards	%	TD	Int
1985	Tampa Bay	138	72	935	52.2	3	8
1986	Tampa Bay	363	195	2,282	53.7	8	13
1987	San Francisco	69	37	570	53.6	10	0
1988	San Francisco	101	54	680	53.5	3	3
1989	San Francisco	92	64	1,001	69.6	8	3
1990	San Francisco	62	38	427	61.3	2	0
1991	San Francisco	279	180	2,517	64.5	17	8
1992	San Francisco	402	268	3,465	66.7	25	7
1993	San Francisco	462	314	4,023	68.0	29	16
1994	San Francisco	461	324	3,969	70.3	35	10
NFL Totals		2,429	1,546	19,869	63.6	140	68

Where to Write
Steve Young

Mr. Steve Young
c/o San Francisco 49ers
4949 Centennial Blvd.
Santa Clara, CA 95054

Index